THE SUBSTANCE & THE SHADOW

CAPTURING THE SPIRIT OF SOUTHWESTERN COLORADO
A PICTORIAL HISTORY 1880s-1920s

Duane A. Smith with Kendall Blanchard

WESTERN REFLECTIONS
PUBLISHING COMPANY

This book is number

ᴗ58

of a limited edition of 1,000

Published by: Western Reflections Publishing Co. • PO Box 710 • Ouray, CO 81427
Design by SJS Design (Susan Smilanic)

ISBN: 1-890437-56-5
First Edition

Dedicated to

Morley and Arthur Ballantine

and their family

in recognition

of their generous support

of the Center of Southwest Studies

TABLE OF CONTENTS

TRIBUTE TO THE BALLANTINES

The new Center of Southwest Studies at Fort Lewis College is a wonderful dream coming true. This phenomenal 50,000 square feet structure features an architectural style that is consistent with the rest of the campus. Its rugged, sturdy, light tan stone walls and total design give the building a distinctively Southwestern look and reflect the Native American and Hispanic heritage that is central to the mission of the Center. The facility contains a museum, a gift shop, a large rotunda, a library, a large area designed for archiving the many holdings of the Center, laboratories, offices, and a state-of-the-art lecture hall, as well as other spaces appropriate to the operation of an instructional facility.

The Center of Southwest Studies is a multi-functional facility and program. It is a place where scholars from Fort Lewis, the region, and across the country can come to work on research related to the Greater Southwest. Its archives, library, laboratories, and professional expertise facilitate this research. Ultimately the national and international reputation of the Center and that of Fort Lewis College in general will be well served by the research and publications that the new facility will spawn.

The Center has a major instructional function. The Fort Lewis College anthropologists, historians, and members of the Department of Southwest Studies will be housed in the new facility. Their principal commitment is to teaching and providing a high-quality learning experience for Fort Lewis College students. The activities and general ambiance of the Center will enrich that learning experience.

The mission of the Center also includes a major service component. The director of the Center, the staff, and other faculty connected with the new facility and its programs are committed to working with the larger community. The Center's principal responsibility in this area is that of extended education, using its resources to help create a better understanding of the geology and prehistory of the Southwest, its history, its many peoples and cultures, its importance to contemporary American history, and its future.

Perhaps most importantly, the Center functions as a symbol of what is special about Fort Lewis College. It is a statement about the College's commitment to the region, its authority on issues related to the greater Southwest, and its role in bringing a diversity of peoples, cultures, and ideas together to solve common problems. The Center of Southwest Studies is, in many ways, a physical manifestation of the essential Fort Lewis College mission. As historian and former Center director Duane Smith has said:

The new Center of Southwest Studies provides a bridge to the greater community beyond the College, a door to the past, and a window to the future. The opening of the new building is a propitious moment.

This Center that was once a dream and then became a reality not an accident. It happened because of the hard work and enerosity of many people: individual faculty and staff at Fort ewis College, donors of all kinds, and the support of the State f Colorado. However, one family deserves more credit than any ther; this is the Morley and Arthur Ballantine family. Their npact on and importance to this project are immeasurable. As ormer Fort Lewis College, President Joel Jones has said, with ference to his ten years of service to the College:

> ...the support, both monetary and advisory, proffered by the Ballantine family proved fundamentally critical to the success of all of our major fundraising efforts. Without their support we would have faced a nearly insurmountable challenge in the capital campaign for the Center of Southwest Studies. The family commitment to the welfare of this region, the cause of higher education in general, and the specific well-being of Fort Lewis College has been exemplary for decades.

Indeed, few families have had a greater impact on the last fty years of Durango history and on Fort Lewis College than ave the Ballantines. On July 1, 1952, Arthur Ballantine, r. and his wife Morley Cowles Ballantine purchased the *Herald-Democrat* and the *Durango News*, merging them into he *Durango Herald-News*, which shortly thereafter became he *Durango Herald*. The subsequent success of the

newspaper, the growth of Durango, and the coming-of-age of Fort Lewis College are in many ways a reflection of the talents, energy, and ambitions of the Ballantine family. The new Center of Southwest Studies at Fort Lewis symbolizes both what is special about the College and the importance of the impact that the Ballantines have had on the region.

The story of the Ballantines in Durango is one filled with great accomplishments, a commitment to education, a passion for the arts, and a deep sense of history. Both Morley and Arthur came from families who had distinguished themselves in many ways, but particularly by their leadership in education, public life, and the newspaper business. They brought their talents and commitments to Durango, having chosen the community because of its beauty, their belief that the region had a great future, and their sense that the quality of life in any community is enhanced significantly by its having an institution of higher learning. In 1952, Fort Lewis was a two-year school and still located on the old Hesperus campus. However, the Ballantines could see an exciting future for the College and were among those who ultimately played a key role in making that future happen.

The accomplishments of the Ballantines and their contributions to the community have been many and varied. Both Arthur and Morley are known for their love of the humanities, their passion for reading, and their belief in and solid support for education. Arthur Ballantine, although technically a journalist, was a serious history scholar whose broad knowledge and depth of understanding was sustained by a life-long habit of reading. According to the Ballantine children, he went nowhere without a book. In fact, daughter

Elizabeth tells of horse-back riding trips during which her father would be lost in the pages of a history book while bouncing along astride some frisky trotter.

The Ballantines are also known for their generosity, willingness to invest their time and money in support of community causes, and their broad commitment to philanthropy. Fort Lewis College has been one of the prime benefactors of the Ballantine goodwill. Arthur was one of the original forces behind the organization of the Fort Lewis College Foundation. Both Morley and Arthur have made sizeable donations to the College and assumed significant leadership roles on the Foundation Board. In addition, they have also made notable contributions to other educational foundations and institutions, including the University of Denver and Simpson College.

Because of their many contributions and their active involvement in the life of the city, region, and state, the Ballantines have been the recipients of many awards and recognitions. Arthur received the University of Colorado Regents Distinguished Service Award, and Fort Lewis College has recognized Arthur and Morley with its Distinguished Service Award. Just this year, Morley was selected to receive Colorado's Outstanding Philanthropist Award from the National Philanthropy Day organization.

When Arthur Ballantine, Jr. passed away in 1975, Colorado, Durango, and Fort Lewis College lost a great thinker, journalist, philanthropist, and friend. Since that time, Morley has continued to sustain the growth and influence of the *Durango Herald* enterprise and invest her time, money, and energy in support of those causes she feel most important to the life of the larger community. Fortunately, Fort Lewis College remains at the top of that list.

The Ballantine children are also major assets to Durango, Southwest Colorado, and Fort Lewis. Richard, Bill, Helen and Elizabeth have each in their own ways distinguished themselves and continued the family tradition of service, education, and philanthropy.

Richard Ballantine grew up in Durango but, having a yen for California, went off to college at Stanford, where he graduated with a baccalaureate degree in history. Subsequently, he returned to Colorado and moved to Denver, where he got into the farming business. It was during these years that he met his wife Mary Lyn, who was also living in Denver at that time and working as a paralegal. Richard and Mary Lyn married in 1980 and moved to Durango. Shortly thereafter, Richard assumed the role of publisher at the *Herald* and began building a reputation of his own as another in the long line of Ballantine-Cowles distinguished journalists. Among the many awards and recognitions that his success has earned for him was his selection as the Colorado Newspaper Person of the Year by the Colorado Press Association in 1997.

Over the past two decades Richard and Mary Lyn have been actively involved in the life of the community and continue to support a variety of philanthropic causes. One of those is Fort Lewis College. Among their many contributions to the College is their recent gift to the Center of Southwest Studies of the finest and largest collection of Native American weavings in the world. This collection, known as the Durango Collection, was built by Mark Winters and the late H. Jackson Clark. It will play a major role in creating a national visibility for the Center and the College. According to Andrew Gulliford, the director of the new Center,

> ...the centerpiece of the Centers museum will be the magnificent Durango Collection which represents almost eight centuries of Southwestern weaving. From a rare Ancestral Puebloan blanket in excellent condition (only three such 800-year old blankets are known to exist) to a womans two piece dress from about 1750 that is the oldest known Navajo textile in existence, the 250 piece Durango Collection is a major resource for Fort Lewis College. We expect that the weavings will be visited by students, collectors, research curators, and numerous national and international tourists. Generations of Fort Lewis students and visitors to Durango will be enthralled by the depth and breadth of the collection

In addition to giving the collection to the College, Richard and Mary Lyn have established an endowment to be used to cover the cost of managing and curating the collection.

Bill Ballantine also grew up in Durango, went to prep school, and eventually matriculated to the University of Washington. It was there he took a degree in political science and ultimately chose to settle in the Seattle area. Bill developed a successful career of his own as an art dealer, real estate developer, and venture capitalist. Currently, Bill stays busy researching and investing in high-tech start-up companies. However, consistent with the Ballantine passion for philanthropy, he still finds time to devote to public service and contribute to causes he believes are important. A lover of sculpture and outdoor public art, Bill has contributed a number of significant pieces to the community of Kirkland, the suburb of Seattle he calls home. He has continued to support Fort Lewis College. Most recently, Bill, investing his own time and money, has managed a process that is leading to the donation of as many as nine large outdoor sculptures to Fort Lewis College. These are to be placed across the center of the campus and promise to add a new and important artistic flare to the Fort Lewis College ambiance.

Helen Ballantine also went off to college, but went East as opposed to West. She began her academic career at Kirkland College, which later merged with and became part of Hamilton College. From here, she transferred to and graduated from Duke University. During her years at Duke she re-established a friendship with and eventually married a young man from her hometown of Durango, Edward Healy. After Edward finished law school at Duke the couple moved to Wichita, Kansas, where he joined the family law firm and became one of the citys most highly respected attorneys. Helen and Ed are active in community service, support a variety of charitable organizations, and share in the Ballantine family's love of and commitment to Fort Lewis College.

Elizabeth Ballantine matriculated to Barnard College after she graduated from high school but transferred to Yale in the first year that Yale changed its admission's policy to include women. Eventually, Elizabeth did her undergraduate work and graduate work at Yale, taking her PhD in Russian Studies. In the process of establishing herself as a scholar and writer, Elizabeth's inherited passion for journalism pulled her into the newspaper business and she went to Des Moines to work for the *Register*. While at the *Register*, she met and married another journalist, Paul Leavitt. When Gannett bought the *Des Moines Register*, Paul was offered position as editor with the Gannetts major paper, *USA Today*, and they moved to Washington. Elizabeth returned to school, this time taking a law degree at American University. Subsequently, she has held several positions in the Washington area and has consulted with a variety of law firms. Using her academic training and extensive travel and international connections, she has specialized in helping American companies broaden their global perspectives, operations, and visibility. Elizabeth and Paul have continued the Ballantine tradition of traveling widely, writing, and supporting educational causes. Like her siblings, Elizabeth has not forgotten Durango and remains a strong supporter and good friend of Fort Lewis College.

In sum, the Ballantine family tradition has become an important part of the Durango and Fort Lewis College traditions. Mary Jane Clark, a Durango businesswoman, community leader, and active supporter of the College speaks for many of her fellow citizens when she notes: Our community was indeed fortunate the day the Ballantine family chose to move to Durango. In innumerable ways they have made Durango a better place to live. The Fort Lewis College community echoes these sentiments. As the College's Vice President for Finance, Robert Dolphin, has said,

It is seldom that a donor has the opportunity to make a significant impact on the development and future of a college. I believe that the Ballantine family with their original contribution that funded the establishment of the Center of Southwest Studies, their recent contributions to the building fund, their gift of the Durango Collection, and Morley leadership in chairing the capital campaign have made a lasting contribution that will enhance the national reputation of Fort Lewis College. Their role in this achievement will be recognized throughout the history of the College.

The dedication of this collection of photographs to the Ballantines is an effort to say thank you and recognize a family whose contributions to Fort Lewis College have made a monumental difference in the look and reputation of the institution. While this gesture is inadequate in many ways, it is hoped it will at least put into perspective the vital importance of the Ballantine investment in the new Center of Southwest Studies and of their continued support of its programs. They have played the leading role in this drama of a dream come true. Without their participation the dream would still be but a dream.

Kendall Blanchard

September 2000

"It seemed not so wild a dream"

The Center of Southwest Studies

The Animas Valley has witnessed the entire saga of the American West over the past 2,200 years. From the hunters and gatherers who tramped along over its land to the tourists who raft down the stream that gives the valley life, the story passes in review. This can be said of few other places, if any, in the United States.

That heritage makes the perfect setting for the Center of Southwest Studies. In the words of the Roman statesman and philosopher, Marcus Tullius Cicero, words themselves written more than 2,000 years ago, "History is the witness that testifies to the passing of time; it illumines reality, vitalizes memory, provides guidance in daily life, and brings us tidings of antiquity." Probably no better statement of the Center's purpose for collecting, preserving and displaying history could be written.

The Southwest Center's history, of course, is not that long. It dates from the early 1960s when Fort Lewis College was evolving from a two-year junior college into a four-year liberal arts institution. Four people were instrumental in its creation—newspaper publishers Arthur and Morley Ballantine, college president John Reed, and history professor Robert Delaney.

The friendly atmosphere of evening get-togethers provided the background for initial discussions. Morley fondly remembered one of those times.

Bob and Arthur were good friends and shared so many of the same interests, and one of them, of course, was the history of the Southwest. They had wonderful times discussing the boundaries of the Southwest. Bob had spent time in Mexico, and he'd spent time in Spain, so he had a large sense of it, and Arthur enjoyed all of the history of this part of the world. So it was a larger vision of geography rather than a smaller one. There was so much being discovered and thought about and discussed that they felt it was necessary to have a repository, a place where scholars could come and look at what existed.

From the beginning came the spark, the concept.

Bob Delaney elaborated a little more in his recollections of those events. Arthur asked him, if Fort Lewis becomes a four-year school, "can you think of something that would enhance its stature and be unique among the four year colleges." Arthur then elaborated, Bob recalled.

'Morley and I would be willing to fund the initial stages and I would try to get other donors to join in on the funding.' I replied, 'let me mull that over for a while and will get back with you soon.' Soon during another evening session, I told Arthur and Morley that I thought a research center devoted to collecting documents and artifacts of the greater southwest and making them available for scholars and other interested persons would be good for Fort Lewis College. The Ballantines thought it was a good idea.

The next step was to present the idea to President John Reed. At the same time, outreach was made to the community at large, and Neil Camp, banker and son of a pioneer family, joined in the discussions. He was "always very supportive," Bob recalled.

President Reed also liked the concept. "Enthusiastic" about it said Morley laughing. He took it to the next step, a meeting of the State Board of Agriculture, for their approval. At this time the name, the Center of Southwest Studies, was born. The State Board approved, and the Center was launched.

The Ballantines provided the "seed" money, in the late spring of 1964, that allowed Delaney to reduce his teaching load to part time and assume the directorship of the Center, a position he held until retiring in 1986. The next step was to provide a place for the Center. A temporary addition was constructed to the academic building, now Brendt Hall. Temporary structures have ways of becoming permanent on college campuses, and that "temporary" room now houses the Vice President of Student Affairs office. Despite President Reed's background as a botanist, and his known love for trees, one had to be cut down. Where it once stood became the huge lazy-Susan-style table that for the next few years was a feature of the Center.

With John Reed's backing, "with his whole heart and soul," the Center was established as a separate entry, not "a part of any division or department of Fort Lewis College. Once the Center found a home, collections started to arrive. Director Delaney promoted the Center through local television programs, newspaper articles, speeches to groups around the town and region, and, for several summers, with a "Southwest Days" celebration on campus.

The result was that, with increasing numbers of documentary collections, books, and material collections, the Center soon outgrew its temporary home. Fortunately, plans were being made to build a new library, and Boulder architect, James Hunter, began planning the third floor as the new Southwest Center. When the building opened in 1967, the public saw a striking mosaic map of the Four Corners region in a Spanish décor reading and research room. Exhibit cases lined the wall. A conference room and offices completed the arrangements.

Remembering that map brought back memories to Bob about the trials of putting it in place.

We started out cutting those little tiles and making the river flow like a river. We got awfully tired of that. The rivers went at right angles because we could cut the tiles in half a lot easier. The Mosaic was laid out on the floor of the library and we all helped, Ria (Delaney) and I and Mrs. Marguerite Norton (the Center's first librarian and archivist). Everybody carried them up and the workmen put them on the wall by the fireplace and glue them on. The only thing that ever happened, some students liked to take their initials (letters) off (the map), and we had to replace a few letters now and then.

It proved worth the effort, that map has been a featured attraction for visitors.

When the Center moved into its new location, it could better fulfill its three "roles:" in education, developing archives, and as a museum. Eventually, out of the offering of courses on the southwest, a new major emerged, Southwest Studies. Stressing an interdisciplinary curriculum, both the major and the Center focused on the entire southwest, with particular emphasis placed on the Four Corners states. The hope since John Reed's days had always been that the Center would emerge as the college's "crown jewel."

Within the next two decades, the Center's holdings became one of the best collections in Colorado. Museum exhibit space, however, remained tight even in the library location, and as books and collections expanded, discussion returned to a dream of the 1960s, a separate Southwest Center building. Eventually, books pushed most of the collections out of the library, and they had to be stored off campus. Exhibits were cut back, and the conference room had to be used as an office. Equipment was stored in research space, which shrank by placing some of the exhibit cases there to at least partially provide something for the public to see.

Finally, in the mid-nineties, dreams started to become reality. Plans for a building took shape, fund raising was started, a ground breaking held, and enthusiasm mounted as the work started in 1999. A mild winter aided in keeping the Center on schedule, and soon the building started to emerge beyond the hole that became the basement.

The history of the Center had been uneven over its first decades. Staffing and funding had always been less than sufficient to fulfill the goals of the 1960s. Nonetheless, the dream never died. Morley Ballantine summarized it well.

I think the progress of the Center has been uneven in one sense, but it has been a success ongoing. It's grown in academia, and it's been fortunate in having strong directors who taught popular courses students enjoyed so that in the dimension of the mind it grew, although perhaps not physically as a building. Collections all grew so that they were all over town finally, which is where they are today. The Center is one of the first in the nation and probably today one of the biggest in the nation in terms of its collections.

Fort Lewis' Southwest Center was the first in the nation with the concept its founders embraced in the early 1960s. It had fulfilled a dream. As Nathaniel Hawthorne explained in *The Scarlet Letter*, which is equally true for the Center, "It seemed not so wild a dream."

Abraham Lincoln wrote during the Union's dark December days of 1862, "Fellow citizens, we cannot escape history." We cannot. History has much to show us, to teach us. The words of former University of Colorado present, George Norlin, ring as true today as they did seventy years ago. "Who knows only his own generation remains always a child."

The Southwest Center takes its charge of preserving, displaying and educating into a new millennium and the twenty-first century. The past has been but a prologue. Tomorrow's Center will be yesterday's dreams and today's expectations.

Duane A. Smith

September 2000

THE MISTY ROAD OF YESTERDAY

What you are about to see is only the tip of an amazing photographic collection. Within its holdings are photographs featuring a wide range of subjects covering the years from the 1880s into the 1960s with the majority falling in the decades of the 1880s through the 1920s. The main focus viewed the area from the Four Corners through the Montrose/Delta region, but there are other photos from throughout Colorado, and a few beyond.

The photographers who took these photographs lived in Delta and Montrose principally and traveled about recording what they saw as well as taking photos in their studios. Both Montrose and Delta had photographers by the decade of the 1890s. Over the years, many of their collections eventually came to be gathered in Montrose's Main Street Photography under the guidance of Dexter Walker. These, then, were the ones that were purchased by the Center of Southwest Studies.

The Colorado poet, Thomas Hornsby Ferril wrote in his fascinating poem "Judging from the Tracks,"

> Man and his watchful spirit lately walked   This misty road...at least the man is sure, Because he made his tracks so visible, as if he must have felt they would endure.

These Colorado photographers captured those tracks for nearly a century starting when they were very dim and ending when they could be found everywhere.

That is the beauty of this collection, its range in span, subjects, and scope. Much of what you are about to see is as gone as yesteryears' sunsets. Perhaps they are only dimly remembered, fortunately, they have been captured for eternity in glass plate and film. Savor and enjoy.

THEY BELIEVED

A PHOTOGRAPHIC HISTORY OF SOUTHWESTERN COLORADO, 1880s-1920s

Flying over the winter-locked San Juans, David Lavender described what he saw, "The awesome sight was the high-country snow, rolling, dipping, swelling, slit by chasms and punctured by giant fists of rock." The San Juans are awesome in winter or any season. Lizard Head.

The "bear eating out of the honey pot" has attracted photographers to Bear Mountain for over a century..

Mt. Wilson and Wilson Peak, two of the San Juans' 14,000 foot mountains.

To the north of the San Juans lies rich farm land in the Uncompahgre Valley.

BRIDAL VEIL FALLS

Bridal Veil Falls plunges 365 feet with an electric power plant at its top.

Puny humans faced nature in the San Juans. Snow slides, floods, snow, and lightning have killed and injured far more people than other accidents. The Telluride flood of 1909.

The Black Canyon of the Gunnison is Colorado's deepest gorge, 3,000 feet of sheer wall at its highest point. The Denver & Rio Grande built a line through it in 1882.

The first settlers found a variety of animals throughout the region, none more fascinating than bighorn sheep.

People arrived 2,000 or more years ago, hunting and gathering. Eventually they farmed, built villages, and then left leaving behind a mysterious heritage. Balcony House, Mesa Verde National Park.

The Anasazi, or Ancestral Pueblo people, departed in the late thirteenth century. This tower found at Hovenweep, marked what they had once called home.

The Utes called this entire region home by the time Europeans arrived. This photo of the famous Ute leader Ouray was taken in Washington, D.C. He died in 1880, as the government prepared to remove most of the Utes from Colorado.

Ouray and his wife Chipeta. Ouray, a skillful negotiator, gained fame from his peace efforts. Chipeta, his support throughout the trials of the 1870s, outlived him by forty-four years.

Buckskin Charlie, a good friend of Ouray, and a Southern Ute leader. The last traditional leader of the Capote band, he lived until 1936.

Little Jim posed at a studio, probably in Montrose.

Spanish prospectors and miners arrived in the eighteenth century; Americans came after the 1859 Pike's Peak gold rush. As that one-time prospector, Mark Twain, portrayed mining fever: "By and by I was smitten with silver fever. Plainly his was the road to fortune."

The highest mining region in the United States, the San Juans were opened permanently and settled by miners starting in the 1870s. The Silver Ledge Mill in the foreground with the little camp of Chattanooga beyond.

The mining era had faded into history, when this photo of Guston and Red Mountain #2 were taken. In the 1880s this area boomed as a silver district.

SAVAGE BASIN FROM SMUGGLER MINE

Savage Basin was home to the famous Tomboy Mine. It produced over $22,000,000 in gold from 1899-1923.

GRAND TURK VEIN
TIDAL WAVE MINE
OPHIR COLO.

There was an old saying, "the higher the silver mine, the richer the ore." Above Ophir was the Tidal Wave Mine, but not a lot of rich ore. Prospectors followed their dream to some nearly inaccessible places.

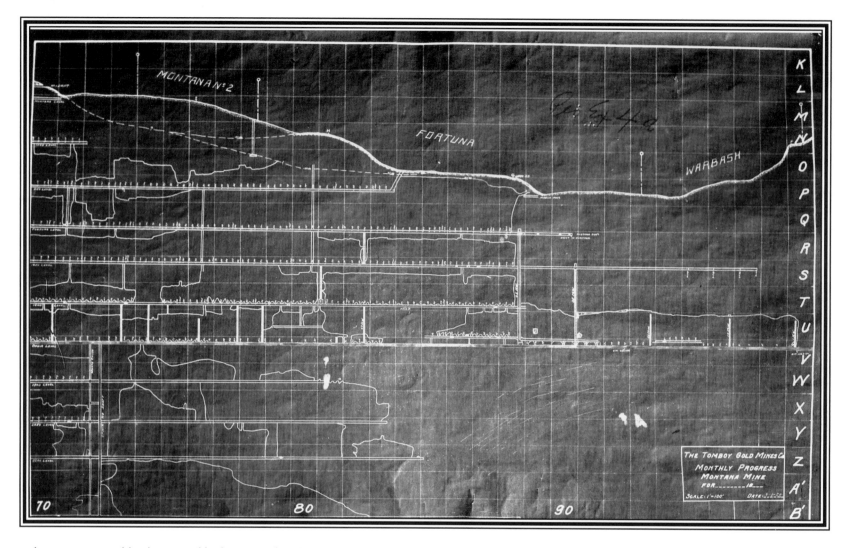

The prospector and his burro quickly disappeared in the wake of companies and corporation mining. This map of part of the Tomboy workings shows why it took money and skill to operate in the San Juans.

Interior mine photographs were a rarity in the nineteenth century. Flash powder and mine timbers did not produce a good mix. Tidal Wave Mine.

Skilled miners made the San Juans prosper. For $3 or $3.50 a day, they risked their lives in a labor intensive, dangerous occupation. Even the best of them never guaranteed a mine's success, however.

Above ground workers toiled longer hours but were equally as important to a mine's success as their underground contemporaries. Someone had to sharpen the drill bits, butt mine timbers, operate the hoist, and do a score of other jobs.

Most San Juan mines were small operations, with the owner and a few miners scratching out hopes and dreams. They lasted a season or two or three, then reality ended the hope. As Martin Luther commented, "Satan deludes many in mines."

Vital members of any mine crew, the cooks received higher pay. Poor ones might be driven right off the mountain, and a mine manager knew he needed to find the best available. They generally were men.

x

San Juan miners pioneered in the use of tramways and electricity. The Tomboy tram terminal that ran to a mill and railroad siding is pictured.

To overcome distance, elevation, and the cost of freighting, trams proved invaluable. Some ran for as long as four or five miles from mine to valley floor. Tomboy tram.

The trail of the miners could be followed by tree stumps, mine dumps, and abandoned buildings. The environmental impact of all this would be considered a century later.

The Gold King operation, above Ophir, was the first to use A.C. electrical power under the guidance of Lucien L. Nunn. It also offered a magnificent view of the mountains.

On the road to the Tomboy Mine. Harriet Backus, in her Tomboy Bride, called this "the tunnel of love." The caption on the back of the photo simply said "social tunnel."

Powder train going up the Smuggler trail to the mine of the same name. Giant powder, or dynamite, eased the work of the miner but presented new problems and dangers as well.

ON THE TRAIL TO THE TIDAL WAVE MINE
OPHIR, COLO.

Without these mountain trails, the miners could not have stayed in the San Juans. Freighting became a major business in Ouray, Silverton, Telluride, and every other community.

The work that it took to move materials up these trails is clearly shown. It demanded skill and long hours to move from valley floor to mine portal.

Mud, snow, and altitude hampered animals and men. An unidentified photo, probably in the Ouray area. Winter freighting was more costly and dangerous.

Tram buckets could carry 250 or more pounds and ran on gravity with loaded buckets going down and hauling empty ones up. Men and supplies could be moved as well, but it took courage to ride one.

The stage coach brought the first investors, tourists, and others into the region, The railroad replaced it whenever possible. The last stage between Ouray and Montrose, August 23, 1887.

When the railroad finally penetrated the San Juans in the 1880s and 1890s, it was considered an engineering marvel. None more so than the famous Ophir Loop on the Rio Grande Southern.

The mining West was an urban West. Mines and miners, in theory, had money, and they certainly had needs. So folks came to "mine the miners" in some beautiful locations. Silverton.

OFFICE OF TIDAL WAVE MINE
OPHIR COLO.

The numerous mining camps were smaller in population and business district, and generally higher in elevation and more isolated than their neighbors, the mining towns. Ophir.

Telluride boomed after the coming of the railroad in 1891. Three of the richest San Juan mines were located nearby. Labor violence rocked the community in 1903-04.

Red Mountain, with its National Bell Mine, suffered the fate of many mining communities. It burned in August 1892. The "Sky City" arose from the ashes, but only as a shadow of its former self.

The mining town of Ouray has few rivals for the beauty of its setting. The scenery, hot springs, and mining attracted tourists as early as the 1880s.

Mining encouraged others to come. Almost on the heels of the miners, the lumbermen arrived. Saw mills, such as this, operated throughout the region.

Ranchers settled north, west, and south of the mountains and sold their cattle to local butchers. A few drove cattle into the mountains for the summer and sold them there.

Sheep and their herders shared the region with farmers and miners, but not always on a friendly basis.

Steam thrashing machines and crews are a memory of the past. Farmers, along with ranchers, arrived back in the 1870s.

A hearty crop of potatoes from Montrose/Delta fields.

Farming towns grew more slowly than their mining neighbors. The 1900 census-takers counted 1,227 for Montrose, compared to Telluride's 2,446 and Ouray's 2,196. Ten years later Montrose passed them both. Montrose in 1885.

"Here is a land where life is written in water, the West is where the water was and is," wrote poet Thomas Hornsby Ferril. That certainly was true for this corner of Colorado. Drilling for an artesian well.

There never existed enough water in the Uncompahgre Valley for everyone, so the settlers turned to Uncle Sam. Gunnison River water came through a tunnel and canals, in the first federally-sponsored reclamation project in Colorado.

President William Howard Taft arrived on September 23, 1909, to officially inaugurate the Uncompahgre project. The next April, he threw out the first ball to start the major league baseball season, thereby starting a tradition which lasted for decades.

People moving west tried to recreate, as much as possible, the life they left behind. Telluride celebrated July 4th with a firemen's race. Betting and town pride rode on the outcome.

Nothing like an opera house to show the world that Montrose had "arrived," even if opera might never be sung there. The local company of the Colorado National Guard proudly stands at attention.

RJS MULE PACK TRAIN.

The main street of a farming or mining town had specialized businesses, such as "gent's furnishings," drug store, jeweler, bank, hotel, and grocery among those found in Telluride. Another fact that kept these towns alive, designation as the county seat—Telluride, Ouray, Silverton, Durango, Montrose, Delta. Only Rico lost that designation.

A Montrose parade poses for a photo, including a dog and horse-drawn fire trucks.

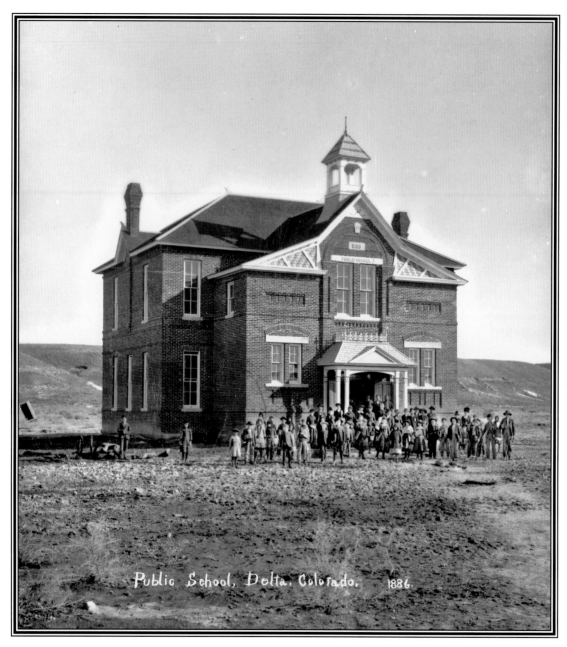

Public School, Delta. Colorado. 1886.

Schools were near and dear to the hearts of most people, a sure sign of civilization. This 1886 Delta photo probably includes the entire student body.

A community with a high school could boast indeed, but it would not be until 1920 that half the high school age students actually went that far. Durango opened this building in 1916.

What was a parade without floats? What was a float without young girls promoting Montrose's pioneer Lathrop Hardware store? It had been started as a farm equipment and hardware store.

Americans joined lodges and other organizations in huge numbers in the nineteenth century. They provided an entry into the community, friendship, ritual, and a sense of belonging. Ridgway's Woodmen of the World proudly smile. Obviously, women had a role in whatever they are celebrating.

Women's athletics astounded some people at the turn-of-the-century and generated their share of controversy. Montrose's basketball players seem a solemn group.

A local band provided a sign of culture, arriving along with entertainment from a concert in the city park to a chivaree for a newly-married couple.

Here was something that attracted attention, a "balloon dare devil."

Back in September 1909, a flood cut off Telluride's rail service. The town nearly ran out of beer before this pack train arrived proudly advertising its precious cargo. The town's thirty-three saloons could relax.

When the automobile arrived, an era was ending. Soon the livery stable, "old dobbin," and the carriage would be gone, and companies would promote themselves on this new invention.

The world was rushing in as it never had before. By 1914, world war had broken out in Europe and San Juaners could read all about it in their newspapers. By 1918, American boys were lining up to "go over there."

Cars now paraded down Main Street as the "roaring" twenties roared in. What a transformation in the past forty years! Telluride native David Lavender captured why pioneers came and remained. In his Red Mountain he wrote, "What made them go was a sort of urge, a frame of mine,... That's what built Red Mountain. They believed."